Mac
That Work

by Kim Borland

PEARSON

Glenview, Illinois
Boston, Massachusetts
Chandler, Arizona
New York, New York

Photographs
Every effort has been made to secure permission and provide appropriate credit for photographic material. The publisher deeply regrets any omission and pledges to correct errors called to its attention in subsequent editions.

Photographs: Photo locators denoted as follows: Cover (CVR), Cover Flaps (FP); Top (T), Center (C), Bottom (B), Left (L), Right (R), Background (Bkgd).

CVR: Richard Leeney/Dorling Kindersley, Ltd.

FP1: Tim Ridley/Dorling Kindersley, Ltd.; 1: Dmitry Kalinovsky/Shutterstock; 2: Stockbyte/Getty Images; 3: Yury Gubin/Fotolia; 4–5: Dorling Kindersley, Ltd.; 6: Richard Leeney/Dorling Kindersley, Ltd.; 7: Tim Ridley/Dorling Kindersley, Ltd.; 8: Richard Leeney/Dorling Kindersley, Ltd.; 9T: Mike Dunning/Dorling Kindersley, Ltd.; 9B: Richard Leeney/Dorling Kindersley, Ltd.; 10: Guy Farrow/Dorling Kindersley, Ltd.; 11: Hoda Bogdan/Fotolia; 12: Tim Ridley/Dorling Kindersley, Ltd.; 13: Dmitry Kalinovsky/Shutterstock; 14: Amc/Alamy; 15: 123RF; FP5: Dorling Kindersley, Ltd.; FP6TL: Dmitry Kalinovsky/Shutterstock; FP6TR: Dorling Kindersley, Ltd.; FP6B: Amc/Alamy.

ISBN-13: 978-0-328-61758-6
ISBN-10: 0-328-61758-X

11 16

Machines That Work

by Kim Borland

PEARSON

Glenview, Illinois
Boston, Massachusetts
Chandler, Arizona
New York, New York

Photographs
Every effort has been made to secure permission and provide appropriate credit for photographic material. The publisher deeply regrets any omission and pledges to correct errors called to its attention in subsequent editions.

Photographs: Photo locators denoted as follows: Cover (CVR), Cover Flaps (FP); Top (T), Center (C), Bottom (B), Left (L), Right (R), Background (Bkgd).

CVR: Richard Leeney/Dorling Kindersley, Ltd.

FP1: Tim Ridley/Dorling Kindersley, Ltd.; 1: Dmitry Kalinovsky/Shutterstock; 2: Stockbyte/Getty Images; 3: Yury Gubin/Fotolia; 4–5: Dorling Kindersley, Ltd.; 6: Richard Leeney/Dorling Kindersley, Ltd.; 7: Tim Ridley/Dorling Kindersley, Ltd.; 8: Richard Leeney/Dorling Kindersley, Ltd.; 9T: Mike Dunning/Dorling Kindersley, Ltd.; 9B: Richard Leeney/Dorling Kindersley, Ltd.; 10: Guy Farrow/Dorling Kindersley, Ltd.; 11: Hoda Bogdan/Fotolia; 12: Tim Ridley/Dorling Kindersley, Ltd.; 13: Dmitry Kalinovsky/Shutterstock; 14: Amc/Alamy; 15: 123RF; FP5: Dorling Kindersley, Ltd.; FP6TL: Dmitry Kalinovsky/Shutterstock; FP6TR: Dorling Kindersley, Ltd.; FP6B: Amc/Alamy.

ISBN-13: 978-0-328-61758-6
ISBN-10: 0-328-61758-X

11 16

What You Already Know

Technology is using science to solve problems. Technology changes over time. Technology helps people.

Tools and machines are kinds of technology. They help people do work.

Tools and machines are used to farm. They are used to build. Tools and machines are also used to communicate.

A computer is a tool we use to communicate.

Simple machines are tools that have few or no moving parts. People use them to do different kinds of work. Wedges push things apart. Wheels and axles move things. Screws hold things together. Levers lift things. Pulleys and inclined planes move things up and down.

Simple machines help people work. Some big machines are made up of simple machines. The big machines in this book help people build things.

Diggers are used on building sites.

On Site

Have you heard the roar of busy machines at a building site? Have you ever seen the different machines at work?

Many different machines are used to build buildings on a site. You might see machines that dig. You might see machines that pick up and drop or dump. Bulldozers, wheel loaders, and cranes can all help on a building site.

Each big machine has a job to do. Some machines carry. Some machines push. Some machines lift. But they are all alike in an important way. They help people do hard jobs!

These big machines are alike in another way too. They have simple machines in them. Some of these big machines use wheels and axles, screws, levers, and pulleys to do their work.

Diggers

Just say the name and you will know what diggers do. They dig! They dig big holes.

The long arm of the machine bends down to the ground. The bucket digs into the ground. Then it scoops up a load of rocks, sand, and dirt.

The arm lifts the bucket up when it is full. The digger swings around and dumps the load. Then the digger turns back to the hole. It is ready to lift another load!

Diggers have arms that move shovels and buckets.

Dump Trucks

Dump trucks move heavy loads. They carry the loads across building sites. Some dump trucks move loads away from the building site. Other dump trucks bring loads to the building site. Dump trucks can move lots of sand and dirt in and out of the site!

Pedals and levers lift the dump truck's box. The arms push the box up. The back of the dump truck swings open to unload. The load rumbles and tumbles out of the box. It falls onto the ground. Then the driver brings the empty box back down.

A dump truck carries a load.

A dump truck drops a load.

Bulldozers

A bulldozer's job is to make the ground flat. The big blades push heavy loads of stones and dirt over the ground. Other big machines can go to work after a bulldozer has made a place flat and clear.

Bulldozers do not have tires. They move along on tracks.

The tracks are made of many little parts that join together. They spin around to move the machine. The tracks grip the ground. They keep the big machine from sinking into mud.

A bulldozer is a slow-moving machine. But do not let that fool you! It is one of the most powerful machines. It can push very heavy loads!

This bulldozer is clearing a pile of dirt.

Wheel Loaders And Forklifts

Wheel loaders and forklifts move big loads from one place to another. These machines can have different parts on the front. The different parts help move different things. Some have scoops on the front. Some have forks.

All wheel loaders have a moving arm. Levers slide the forks or the scoop under the load. Levers lift the load up off the ground. Then the machine moves the load to a new place.

This forklift picks up the load.

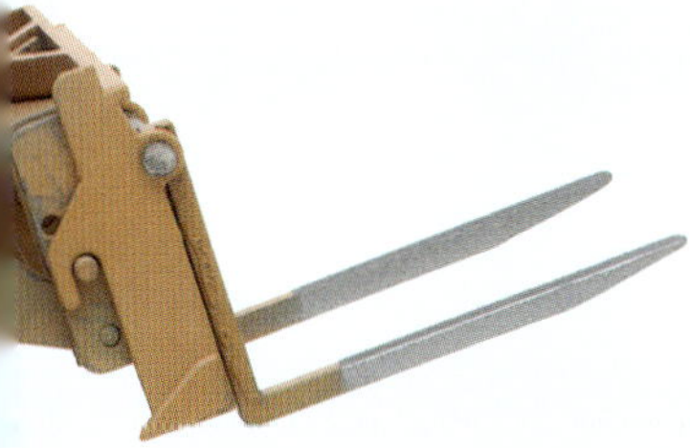

Cranes

Cranes are tall machines that lift and move heavy loads. Cranes use pulleys to move their loads.

Different kinds of cranes do different jobs. Some cranes load things on ships. Some cranes lift things to the tops of tall buildings. Some cranes even lift other cranes!

A crane lifts a house!

Keep your eyes open the next time you pass a building site. Maybe you will see diggers, dump trucks, bulldozers, wheel loaders, and cranes at work. Each one uses simple machines to get the heavy jobs done!

Glossary

bulldozer	a heavy machine used to clear
crane	a tall machine with a long arm that lifts, moves, and lowers
digger	a machine used to make holes in the ground
dump truck	a machine that carries, moves, and unloads
load	something that is carried
site	a place